Reader's Handbook

A Student Guide for Reading and Learning

Great Source Education Group
a Houghton Mifflin Company
Wilmington, Massachusetts

www.greatsource.com

AUTHORS

Laura Robb
Author

Powhatan School, Boyce, Virginia
Laura Robb, author of *Reading Strategies That Work* and *Teaching Reading in Middle School*, has taught language arts at Powhatan School in Boyce, Virginia, for more than 30 years. She is a co-author of the *Reading and Writing Sourcebooks* for grades 3–5 and the *Summer Success: Reading* program. Robb also mentors and coaches teachers in Virginia public schools and speaks at conferences throughout the country on reading and writing.

Margaret Ann Richek
Contributing Author

Northeastern Illinois University, Chicago, Illinois
Margaret Ann Richek is a professor of education at Northeastern Illinois University. Her specialty is the teaching of reading. She is a former teacher in Chicago and the metropolitan Chicago area. She consults extensively for school districts. Her publications include a series of ten co-authored books, *Vocabulary for Achievement* (Grades 3-10), *The World of Words: Vocabulary for College Students*, and a co-authored text, *Reading Problems: Assessment and Teaching Strategies*. Her work is also featured in *Vocabulary Strategies That Boost Students' Reading Comprehension*.

Vicki Spandel
Contributing Author

Writing specialist Vicki Spandel was co-director of the 17-member teaching team that developed the 6-trait model for writing instruction and assessment. She is the author of more than 30 books for students and teachers, including *Daybooks of Critical Reading and Writing* (for grades 3-5) and *Write Traits Classroom Kits*. Vicki has been a language arts teacher, award-winning video producer, technical writer, journalist, freelance editor, and scoring director for numerous writing assessments. As lead trainer for Write Traits, she works as a writing consultant and visiting teacher throughout the country and develops a wide range of instructional materials for use in grades K-12.

Editorial: Developed by Nieman Inc. with Phil LaLeike

Design: Ronan Design: Christine Ronan, Sean O'Neill, Maria Mariottini, and Victoria Mullins

Illustrations: Mike McConnell

Printed in the United States of America
International Standard Book Number: 0–669–49010–5 (hardcover)
2 3 4 5 6 7 8 9—QWT—08 07 06 05 04 03

International Standard Book Number: 0–669–49009–1 (softcover)
2 3 4 5 6 7 8 9—QWT—08 07 06 05 04 03